How to Conquer Anxiety, Worry, Fear & Stress

By Paul Booth

The measure of intelligence is the ability to change.
Albert Einstein

You cannot have a positive life and a negative mind. Joyce Meyer

The mind is everything. We are changed by our thoughts. What you think you become. Buddha

Fortune favours the prepared mind. Louis Pasteur

Yesterday I was clever, so I wanted to change the world. Today I am wise, so I am changing myself. Rumi

When you practice positive affirmations and keep your words and pictures consistent with your goals and dreams, there is nothing that can stop you being the success you are meant to be. Brian Tracy

Your mind only responds to two things: the pictures you make in your head and the words you say to yourself. And they are very easy to change. Marisa Peer

Dedication

I dedicate this book to you the reader. Your willingness to conquer your anxiety, worry, fear and stress tells me that you want more out of life. Being at peace and feeling happy despite the difficulties life throws at us is indeed a challenge, but you are now meeting that challenge, as you implement the instructions in this book.

Thanks

My thanks go to Adriana Silvas whose help and support has made this book possible.

This Mastery Series

My intention is to publish at least 8 books in this Mastery Series. This the 1st one, followed by ... 2) *How to Master Your Confidence and your Courage. 3) How to Master Your Past, Present and Future. 4) How to Master Your Self-Esteem, Self- Control & Responsibility. 5) How to Master Your Relationships. 6) How to Master Your Happiness. 7) How to Master Your Life :Smile, Peace, Love, Appreciation & Enjoyment. 8) How to Master Your Health, Sleep, Energy & Weight.*

Time will tell how this pans out. I will publish them in the order which seems most important to me and hopefully to you.

Disclaimer

This book is intended to help you, conquer anxiety worry fear and stress. It is not intended as a substitute for proper medical treatment. If necessary Always consult with a qualified health professional.

Contents

Introduction ix

Chapter 1: What Controls Your Life? 1

Chapter 2: How Your Mind Works 19

Chapter 3: Training Your Beautiful Mind 36

Chapter 4: How to Conquer Anxiety, Worry, Fear and Stress. 47

Chapter 5: How to Use Your Mind Truths 67

Chapter 6: Mind Truths 73

Chapter 7: Helping Yourself and Helping Others 80

Introduction

So, I'm in a bookshop in Manchester, England and I see a book I really, really, want to own and read. But I'm anxious, embarrassed and worried at what the other people in the shop will think of me. I was scared they would think I was deficient in some way, so I walk away from it and pretend to browse other shelves. When eventually no one's near "the book", I take it off the shelf and examine it. It's perfect, just what I want. Now the only problem is getting it out of the shop. I wait until no one's near the till so they can't see what I've got. I anxiously walk over, hiding the front cover against my leg, just in case anyone should see it. Now there's only the cashier to deal with. What will he think of me? There's no alternative. If I want the book he'll have to see it. I slide it (face down) across the counter to him, and much to my surprise he doesn't look shocked at all. In fact he doesn't say anything. He doesn't even look disapprovingly at me. He even manages a small smile. It goes into a bag and I'm safe. What a relief! No one can see the title now. I walk out of the shop eager to get reading. And the title of this 'terrible', 'embarrassing' book? *How to Stop Worrying and Start Living* by Dale Carnegie.

Anxiety, worry, fear and stress have unfortunately reared their ugly heads throughout my life. My dear mother was brought up by a worrier (my grandma Shaw) and she herself became a worrier. While I'm certainly not blaming my mother for all my anxieties I have no doubt that it influenced me considerably. Finding *How to Stop Worrying and Start Living* was a game changer for me. It introduced me to the world of self-improvement books, and I soaked them up. Over the intervening years I have read many books and bought many courses (cassette courses, CD courses, internet courses). I have bought Brian Tracy lunch. He's an incredible role model. I've attended Tony Robbins' courses in Miami, Hawaii and London and I even became a helper at his courses and many times got to dance on stage with him in front of thousands of crazy Tony Robbins' fans. What a great experience that was. I've recently added blogs and podcasts to my education to help fuel my desire for positive change.

One of the things that has helped me self-develop and self-improve, more than anything else has been doing 'my cards'. For years I've been writing positive statements on 3 by 5 inch cards. As I read a book, or listened to a course or blog I don't take notes, I write what I call Mind Truths instead. For example, one of Dale Carnegie's main principals to stop worrying is to live in day tight compartments. The Mind Truth I have for that is, 'Fear is about tomorrow. I beat it by living today.' Other Mind Truths I have to help me include: 'If I can't influence it, I accept it.' 'I let go of the past. It's over, finished. I move on.' 'I am bigger than my problems and challenges.' 'Action is where the action is. Action diminishes fear. I take action.'

Over the years I have written thousands of individual Mind Truths on hundreds of 3 by 5 cards. The problem was, if I wanted to work on a self-improvement issue, the relevant Mind Truths were scattered among the thousands. This was annoying and it would certainly be a big job to sort them out into subjects. However the stimulus to do this occurred when I thought of how much these Mind Truths would help others, as they have helped me. If I could write a book and get them into people's hands maybe they would be able to conquer *their* fears better and improve and master *their* lives in areas of importance to them. Maybe they wouldn't have to go through the stresses and anxieties I've been through on my journey through life.

When I was younger I was most concerned with 'finding my-self' but I have since learned that the key to life is to 'build myself'. My sincere wish is that you will value this book and use it to conquer your anxiety, worry, fear and stress, and build a more peaceful, stronger, better, happier, more confident and courageous you.

Just so you understand what Mind Truths are, they are statements that you would like to install into your mind, so that they become part of your personality, part of your way of thinking, feeling, and being; part of you. They may already be true, or they may be partly true or they may be something you want to be true and install in your mind. Mind Truths are statements you give to your mind. You expect your mind to process, absorb and embed what you say. So, if you say or read, "I recover quickly from adversity. I am emotionally resilient," there may be some truth in this, and the more you repeat it to yourself (with feeling) the stronger it embeds in your mind and the more it becomes part of you. Mind Truths then become *your* truths. They get stronger and stronger the more you use them. When you do your Mind Truths your mind is stimulated to accept the Mind Truth and put it into operation in your life.

How do you learn anything? By repetition. Repeating Mind Truths is a fun, easy, effective, way of changing (transforming even) your life in the direction you want. In this book you will find many Mind Truths, and guidance in how to use them. But first some background information which will help explain how they work so you can get the best out of them.

CHAPTER 1

~

What Controls Your Life?

Your Most Valuable Asset

What is the most valuable asset you possess? You carry it around with you at all times. It decides how stressed you are, how happy you are, who you fall in love with and marry, what type of house you live in and what car you drive. It decides how many friends you have, how fit and healthy you are, what job or career you pursue, how much money you have, how you live and how you die. It is of course your mind. How do you treat this most important treasured vessel? Do you look after it? Do you feed it well, nourish it, love it? We all know how to look after ourselves physically. We sleep, feed, exercise, wash, shower, clean our teeth. But what do we know about looking after ourselves mentally? Is our physical well-being more important than our mental well-being?

Who are you?

"Who am I?" Is a question many people ask of themselves. Maybe you do too.

You are not your arms or legs or any body part, not even your mind since this is constantly changing . You are not your family or friends. You are not your health or fitness. You are not your age or weight or colour or religion or political persuasion. You are not your skills or talents or experiences or failures or successes. You are not your job or bank balance. *Who* you are is more important than what you *do*, so just who are you?

I find it serves me to think of myself as pure energy. If you were to ask a quantum physicist, he or she would say we are all made up of energy. Energy vibrates, and the rate of vibration changes. Ice, water and steam are all the same thing, but at different vibrations. Different human states have different vibrations too. Anxiety has a very different vibration to relaxation. Boredom has a different vibration to curiosity.

If we categorise emotions as positive or negative, some of the positive ones are: happiness, love, appreciation, enjoyment, peace, patience, fun, kindness, goodness, faith, confidence, generosity, forgiveness, optimism, excitement. Some of the negative ones are: disappointment, sadness, loneliness, frustration, anger, and fear. If you are pure energy, you surely want to be in a positive, pleasant state as much as possible; and when in it, try to stay in it. If you find yourself in a negative, unpleasant state you can make the effort to change it as quickly as possible. This book will help you do that. Unfortunately the predominant energy of many people is lack, struggle, fear and pain. Don't let these people influence you, whether it's the news media, print media, TV, governments, big business, associates, friends or even family. What you focus on you move towards, so focus on designing your own outstanding life. Move towards what *you* want not what others want for you.

Maybe a better way of looking at who we are, is to ask a different question. Instead of asking "Who am I?" ask the question, "Who do I want to be?" and "How do I want to experience my life?" Having decided who you want to be and how you want to experience life, do everything in your power to bring it about.

The Formative Years

If you had been born into a very rich family, who loved and cherished and nurtured and encouraged you, your mind would be full of certain beliefs and truths. And if, unfortunately, you were the unloved, unwanted child of an unemployed drug addict mother, who resented your presence, and constantly criticised you, then your beliefs and truths would be totally different.

When we are born, we are born with a clean sheet, a clean mind, and we start filling it up from day one. In our formative years we don't have any choice as to what goes into our minds to become our truths. It's whatever is happening around us based on our environment and parental activities. Sometimes the things going on around us made us feel frustrated or disappointed or angry or aggressive, and we feel trapped. The good news is that if we want to change, right now, to be in more of the positive states such as happiness, love, confidence, self-esteem, appreciation, we can reprogram our beautiful minds.

Dr Andrew Newberg and Mark Waldman are prolific writers of over twenty books on the brain, and in their book, *How Enlightenment Changes Your Brain*, they state, "From the moment we are born, the human brain has the remarkable ability to constantly change itself. Think about who you are today and who you were a decade ago, or even last year or last month. Although you are the same person, you have learnt new skills, had new experiences, and let go of old beliefs and habits that no longer have relevance in your life." Yes, from today onwards you will continue to change. The issue is to orchestrate your *own* change, rather than random circumstances and other people's agendas changing you. This book will help you change in the direction *you* want: away from anxiety, worry, fear and stress, allowing for peace, happiness, confidence, courage, love, appreciation and enjoyment to be cultivated.

Child Becomes Man

"Give me a child until he is seven and I will show you the man." The origin of this quote is unclear. It could be Aristotle or the Jesuits, but whoever it was, the truth of it is clear; those early days are foundational in building the man or woman of the future.

When you were a child your mind was like a sponge to your environment, and you downloaded what was going on around you. You took in experiences, ideas, thoughts, beliefs, feelings and you became you. But during this time you also took in worries and fears and guilt and shame and jealousies and doubts. Many of these issues from childhood are still with us, even though they don't serve us any more.

They diminish and contract us as human beings. Minimising these negative traits and maximising our wonderful, positive, beautiful traits is the aim of this book.

What Matters Now

Now that you're no longer a child, there is one thing far more important than other people's thoughts and comments, and that is your own thoughts and comments. In other words, it's the words you say to yourself and the pictures you make in your mind, which now matter and influence you and change you. When you were a young child you didn't have the freedom to choose. But now it's different. As a mature, independent thinker you do have the power to choose. You can accept or reject an idea as true or not, simply because you want to. Truths change in you constantly anyway, depending on your circumstances and experiences. Let the good stuff in. Let it change you and your truths for the better. Keep the bad stuff out. Don't let it contaminate you.

As a child you had no choice but to absorb your parents beliefs, but now you can decide for yourself and install new beliefs. As just said, beliefs change in you constantly anyway, so make sure they change to suit you. You can't focus on a positive memory or experience and a negative memory or experience at the same time, so focus on that which serves you. What you focus on expands, so focus on the positive. You can't hold two conflicting thoughts at the same time, for example, "I love travelling by car but we'll probably crash," doesn't work. You can't have sad thoughts and happy thoughts at the same time. Choose happy. You can't be confident and shy at the same time. Choose confidence. Since you can only think one thought at a time, if your thinking is making you stressed or sad or angry, you can substitute it with an uplifting thought. Maybe a thought of peace, happiness or appreciation, or a thought of love.

Past Programming

Some of our past programming may have been debilitating with parents, teachers, friends and associates criticising us and putting us down. Some of our past programming was doubtless very good with caring parents, teachers, friends and associates who encouraged us and expected the best of us. Just one person can have a very positive life changing impact on us, as the story below can testify.

When I went on my first ski instructors course I could barely ski parallel. Out of the 10 classes of 20 skiers in each class I was the third from the bottom in the bottom class.

Fortunately, we had the legend who is Ali Ross as our trainer and he programmed so much confidence into me that I came to believe that I had what it takes. Even though I failed the course, I gave up my job when I got home and drove up to Scotland, where I got a job as a ski instructor. Joy of joys! "My sincere thanks go out to you, Ali. Your faith in me changed my life. You programmed me to believe in myself and my ability to teach skiing."

Who has impacted you for good or bad in the past? As a child you had no option but to be programmed by others. But now it's up to you to take responsibility and decide for yourself what influences you. You can take control of your own programming.

Who Is In Charge of Your Conditioning?

According to Brian Tracy, "We are all conditioned to respond in certain ways either positively or negatively. Unfortunately most of our conditioning has occurred in a random, haphazard way, usually by accident. It's now your job to take full control over your own mental programming, to ensure that the way you automatically respond is consistent with your highest good."

Your past does not equal your future, unless you allow it. Rather, decide what you want and work towards it. This may take responsibility, courage and self-control, but it will be worth it. The effort will be temporary but the results long-lasting.

Negative Emotions

What holds us back in life more than anything else? Negative emotions, especially fear! The worst are fear of failure or loss, fear of rejection or criticism. These are embedded in us as children. Since we are inexperienced, uncoordinated and self-centred at an early age, our parents are constantly correcting us. We learn we don't have the freedom to try things for ourselves, to make our own decisions, to make our own mistakes, live our own lives. We learn frustration and close ourselves down. Negative emotions abound. Unfortunately they can still be with us later in life. Overcome them by conquering anxiety, fear, and stress. Cultivate positive traits such as peace, happiness, love, self-esteem, appreciation, confidence and courage. This will make all the difference.

Our Thoughts

Thoughts are things. Very important things. Thoughts create reality. Our thoughts literally change our world. We must make sure our thoughts serve us well. Every thought you think has a physical reaction in your body. Every word you read fires off neurons in your brain related to that word. When we daydream, our subconscious mind takes over and sends us random thoughts and words and songs and images into our conscious mind. They come and go. This is automatic. A default setting. It takes no effort. It's easy. Bare in mind that you and your thoughts are not the same thing. You are not your thoughts. You are the generator and observer of your thoughts. When debilitating thoughts come up you don't need to believe them or act on them. You are separate from your thoughts.

The beauty of being a human being is that we can override debilitating or even poor thoughts by consciously choosing thoughts and words that nurture us. The most important words you will ever hear are the words you say to yourself either in your head or out loud. By changing the self-talk words, and the pictures in your head to positive, encouraging, upbuilding ones, you reduce fear, you become happier and more confident in life. The self-talk and pictures you make in your head control your feelings. Your feelings control your actions. Your actions control your results. For outstanding results use outstanding self-talk and pictures. Reject negative thoughts and words and pictures, and replace them with life-enhancing ones.

The default setting in our brains is designed to keep us safe and stop us from injuring or killing ourselves; and it does this by constantly looking out for threats. It is like a sentry or a look out, constantly keeping vigil. "Watch out!" "Be careful!" "Is it safe?" "Is there danger here?" It is constantly on guard. If we're not careful we can let this sentry dominate us. Fortunately we can override this by acknowledging that our brain is only doing its job and by focusing on positive things we can do something about.

Many people live in a state of anxiety, worry, fear and stress. If you are to overcome these yourself and you find you are associating with negative people, it may be better to limit your association with them, so their negativity doesn't rub off on you. If you're trying to be happy and are smiling and upbeat when those around you are looking and talking miserably, they may not appreciate your positivity. But don't let them influence you... Don't let them bring you down to their level. Be strong, be confident, be courageous and keep smiling.

What is truth?

The truths that interest us, as we conquer anxiety, worry, fear and stress (while amplifying our positive states), are the personal truths we have internalised. Happily they're not fixed but are flexible. Many of our truths change with time. At one time many people's truth was that the world was flat. That was what they knew. It was a belief, their truth. On a more personal, individual level, if you believe you're not intelligent it will affect your whole life. If your truth is that people are basically honest and kind, you'll interact with them in a very different way to a belief that most people are dishonest and unkind. Which is true? There is no truth here, only opinion and belief. And it can be changed. If you were told as a child you were stupid, it's a rare child that thinks, "No, actually, I'm really intelligent." Now, however you can challenge any truth you want. How intelligent do you think you are now?

Intelligence

The school system when I was growing up equated a good memory to intelligence. Those who memorised the information fed to them got the top marks and the glory. While memory is important there are other intelligences too. Here are a few. Which of these apply to you?

1) Linguistic intelligence – public speakers, journalists, authors, presenters.

2) Spatial intelligence – architects, film directors, sculptors, painters, air traffic controllers.

3) Kinaesthetic intelligence – sportspeople, dancers.

4) Musical intelligence – song writers, musicians, conductors, composers.

5) Interpersonal intelligence – teachers, social workers, interactive influential people, authors, bloggers, podcasters.

6) Naturalistic intelligence – people with an affinity with nature, biologists, botanists, gardeners, animal lovers.

7) Logic/mathematical intelligence – mathematicians, scientists, detectives, programmers.

Of course, we all have different degrees of different intelligences. Some exceptional people such as Leonardo da Vinci excelled in many. The good news is that what we focus on grows, so we can decide which intelligences we want to feed and amplify. Also this means just because we may not be that intelligent in one area, such as maths or languages, doesn't mean we're not intelligent. Look for and focus on your *own* intelligences and strengths.

In their book, *Soar With Your Strengths*, Donald O. Clifton and Paula Nelson write, "Find out what you do well and do more of it; find out what you don't do well and stop doing it." Sounds like good advice to me.

My truth as a child was that I was a great football (soccer to our American friends) player, but when I was kicked off the cub scout football team at the age of 10 my truth changed. At school I was of slight build and a poor runner and not built for rugby (which the school excelled at) so my truth was that I was not sporty. But then I discovered skiing. When I started I was no better than any of my fellow recreational skiers. It was only with time, effort and practice that I became a proficient ski instructor. Since then my truth is that I'm very sporty. So truths can change. The goal of this book is that the truths you hold about yourself and your anxiety, worry, fear and stress, can be conquered, paving the way for positive states such as peace, love, happiness, confidence, courage, appreciation and enjoyment. Use the techniques in this book.

Words Change You

When it comes to your mind, to prove to yourself how the words and pictures in your brain affects your cells and the systems of your body, try this... think of sitting down and waiting for someone to serve you your favourite food dish. It arrives. It looks perfect, just how you like it. It smells wonderful. Then you take a mouthful. Your mouth explodes. It tastes out of this world... Maybe you're now salivating or feeling hungry. Or try the same with a lemon. Imagine picking up a lemon. Feel the peel. Caress it. Smell it. Rub it between your fingers. Pick up a knife and cut into it. Bits of juice spurt out. Smell the flesh of the lemon and feel the sharp odour assaulting your nostrils. Finally bite into it and chew on the flesh and peel. Once again you're probably salivating if you've played full out on this. Note that my words became a sensory experience for you. Words matter. Words cause a sensory experience or physiological responses in your mind and body.

Steer your own life.

There are three things that will completely steer the direction of your mind and life.

1) The words you say to yourself in your head. Your self-talk.

2) The images which are in your head. The pictures you make.

3) The meaning you give to the incidents in your life.

I love the story of the woman who is distraught because her husband and two boys refuse to take their shoes off in the house. They walk over her pride and joy of a beautiful, new, white carpet in the lounge. Every time she sees the dirty footprints she gets upset and stressed, so goes to a psychologist for help on how to change her family's behaviour. The psychologist has her relax and see the beautiful white carpet in her mind's eye. Then he says, "Know this, that the clean white carpet represents the loneliness you feel in your heart. No one loves you. No one comes to see you. No one walks on your white carpet because you are all alone without family or friends." The situation hasn't changed, but the meaning of the situation has. Now a clean carpet means loneliness and a dirty carpet means family, friends and love. She returns home happy, to a dirty carpet. Events themselves don't affect us as much as the meaning we attached to them and the interpretation we put on them.

This can be difficult to get your head around. But it is worth the effort. There is no absolutely fixed meaning to anything in life. It is always affected by the point of view we bring to it.

So what ever happens to us and whatever situation we are in, we give it meaning.

I remember getting sacked from a job I didn't want to get sacked from. I was upset, angry and stressed for a short while, until I changed the meaning and decided to look on it as an opportunity to find a better, more suitable job. I applied myself to this and a short while later, I found such a job. If we can look for and find something positive in a situation, then although nothing has changed externally we feel happier internally. We can always ask ourselves, "What good could come out of this?" Or "What meaning shall I choose that will serve me now?"

The same situation experienced by a group of people will result in a different meaning for each one. Each individual experiences the situation through the filter of their own truths. What we think is reality is only reality for the individual, so reality is personal to you. Everyone's reality is different, which can be a blessing or a curse. Don't expect anyone else to see things the way you do. Don't expect anyone else to see *you*, the way you do. They can't, but that's okay. Your job is to know yourself and be the best you, you can be, while you love them and embrace the differences.

We are all doing the best we can, given our own individual circumstances and truths. Your truths and their truths are changing all the time. Your job is to reject truths that don't serve you and absorb truths that do serve you. If you are not as happy as you want to be and your life is not everything that you dream it could be, the good news is that only one person is responsible and in control of your future. It is you, based on the truths going on in your head.

In the next chapter we'll look at the other two things that steer the direction of your mind and life; the words and pictures in your head. We'll also look at what we can do practically to make positive changes, master our mindsets and master our lives; spending more time in happier, more peaceful, more beautiful, fun, enjoyable states.

CHAPTER 2

❧

How Your Mind Works

*M*y mindset is my most critical element. My mindset is more important than my knowledge, my wealth, my everything... How you form your mindset is critically important. Peter Diamandis

Have you ever upgraded your phone or TV or car? Very likely. We often want the latest version, expecting it to work better and give us more happiness, confidence, pride, pleaesure. But how often do we upgrade our minds with a view to mastering this most valuable and important thing that we possess? Let's not put up with an older, inferior model mind when, with a bit of time, effort and fun, we can create a better, masterful one. You are not stuck with the mind you've got. You can make it better.

As we have seen previously, the truths that we hold in our mind are formed initially in our formative years, especially ages one to seven. However, we do keep changing and are changing constantly. Our minds are malleable and we keep changing and learning right up to the day we die. Many of our present truths and changes have happened in a haphazard way which have not necessarily served us. Now is the time to change our truths for the better, using the technique I call Mind Truths.

When you talk to yourself and encourage yourself with a positive idea or instruction, it's called an affirmation. Affirmations have been around for a long time. An early proponent of affirmations (also known as self-suggestion or auto-suggestion) was Emile Coue (26-2-1857 to 22-7-1926). He was a brilliant French health practitioner who is famous for having his patients frequently repeat, «Every day, in every way, I'm getting better and better." Talking of auto-suggestion, he stated, "It can wound or even kill you if you handle it imprudently and unconsciously. It can, on the contrary, save your life when you know how to employ it consciously."

A more modern proponent of affirmations was Muhammad Ali. He said, "It's the repetition of affirmations that leads to belief. And once that belief becomes a deep conviction, things begin to happen." Things certainly happened for him as he kept telling himself and the world, "I am the greatest."

They can happen for you too, when you develop the skill of using Mind Truths.

As mentioned in the introduction, Mind Truths are statements that you would like to install into your mind, so that they become part of your personality, part of your way of thinking, feeling, and being; part of you. Mind Truths are statements you give to your mind. You expect your mind to process, absorb and embed what you say. There's usually a sliding scale of truth about them already. For example, if you say, "I am bold and courageous," your mind may say something like, "Okay, sometimes you are, sometimes less so." However, as you keep instructing and insisting, "I am bold and courageous," the mind will get the message and you will feel more and more bold and courageous. For this reason, I like to call these statements Mind Truths, since they become truths for you. They steadily grow, amplify and ripen in your mind, the more you use them.

The mind can only focus on one thing at a time, so take advantage of this and have it focus on positive Mind Truths. Try reading a book and having a conversation with someone at the same time. You can switch from one to the other, but not focus on both together. So it is with your conscious mind. So focus on Mind Truths that encourage you, build you up, and change you. Flood your mind with Mind Truths rather than allowing indiscriminate, or debilitating thoughts to randomly pop up in your head and control you.

Since your mind does what you tell it, tell it great things. Since your mind works by repetition, keep repeating great things. Since you are a person of choice, choose to enjoy using Mind Truths. Become good at using Mind Truths. Make it a habit. Decide that Mind Truths will help you eliminate anxiety, worry, fear and stress and move you towards becoming the peaceful, happy, confident, courageous person you want to be.

Be happy. Be thrilled. Be encouraged. Be inspired by yourself. Be a winner. Be successful. Have a great life. You are in control. Don't let your mind take in random or poor instructions from circumstances around you. Take control of your own mind. Be in charge of it. Be your own best friend. Encourage yourself and when fears come up in the way of debilitating words or pictures override them with encouraging words and pictures. Be a loving friend and a great parent to yourself.

Parents And Children

Giving correct instructions to the mind is vital for a good outcome. One of my pet peeves is when I hear parents disciplining their children with instructions such as, "Don't run," "Don't slam the door," "Don't climb up there. You'll fall off and hurt yourself." Can you see the problem? All these instructions put a negative image in the child's mind - exactly what the parent doesn't want. It's no wonder they don't respond or quickly do it again.

How much better to say, "Walk." "Close the door slowly and quietly." "When you're climbing, just be careful." This puts the right images in the child's mind so they're more likely to obey. It's exactly the same when we talk to ourselves. Giving our minds positive instructions moves us toward a positive outcome. The most important person you communicate with is yourself. You have the ability to communicate clearly with yourself through your words and pictures, so your mind will work for you, not against you. It is a skill you can develop with the help of this book.

Two Wolves

As we have seen, Mind Truths are hardly a new idea and there's a lovely American Indian legend which illustrates this. Here's how the story goes...

An old Cherokee is teaching his grandson about life. "A fight is going on inside me," he tells the boy. "It is a terrible fight and it is between two wolves. One is evil. He is anger, envy, sorrow, regret, greed, arrogance, self-pity, guilt, resentment, inferiority, lies, false pride, superiority, and ego." He continued, "The other is good. He is joy, peace, love, hope, serenity, humility, kindness, benevolence, empathy, generosity, truth, compassion, and faith. The same fight is going on inside you and inside every other person too." The grandson thought about it for a minute and then asked his grandfather, "Which wolf will win?" The old Cherokee simply replied, "The one you feed."

Yes, feeding your mind with good, positive, encouraging, life-enhancing words and pictures is what Mind Truths are all about.

Your Subconscious Mind

If your subconscious mind is not encouraging your happiness and it throws up random or repetitive thoughts that scare you and pull you down, what can you do? You can use your conscious mind to override these thoughts and use better, more empowering words and pictures, such as you get here in these Mind Truths. Take control of your conscious mind to feed and update your subconscious mind. Give your conscious mind clear Mind Truths it can grasp and work with. With time and repetition they will be absorbed and accepted by your subconscious mind. Yes, it may take a bit of time, but if you keep telling yourself something such as, "I am enough, I like myself, I love myself," your subconscious mind will start to believe it and you'll start to behave it too.

Our brains are association machines. If I say "banana" to you, you imagine a banana in your mind's eye. If I say "smile", you process that word and maybe smile yourself or imagine someone else smiling. If I say to you, "You are enough, you are kind, and you have a lovely smile," your brain must process it, and it's the same when you say it to yourself. "I am enough. I am kind and I have a lovely smile." Your brain must process it and the more you think and say it, the stronger the impact and the truer it becomes. This is how Mind Truths work.

When you tell yourself something, over and over again, it's going to embed into your mind. It's more important than someone else telling you. For example if you don't think you can do something, but someone says, "You can do it," it may be encouraging, but it doesn't mean you're likely to do it. Alternatively, if someone says, "You can't do that," but you say, "Yes, I can," and you keep telling yourself you can, that's far more effective and powerful, and will likely get results.

If you decide you're pleasing to look at, then it's true. It's your truth, your Mind Truth. If you decide you've got a good sense of humour, then it's true. It's your truth, your Mind Truth. If you decide you're kind and happy and confident and appreciative, etc., etc., well, you get the idea. The Great Universal Truth is, you become what you think about and say to yourself, most of the time. Decide to conquer your anxiety, worry, fear and stress using the Mind Truths in this book.

Obsolete Thoughts

We are not our thoughts and we certainly don't need to believe every thought that comes up into our head. Many of our thoughts are obsolete thoughts from the past, which are no longer valid and no longer serve us. Allow these debilitating thoughts to come and go. We can override them and move them along more quickly by focusing on thoughts that do serve us. Doing the Mind Truths in this book, will seed your mind with thoughts that serve you, until they blossom and dominate your thinking. I use Mind Truths all the time. When I catch myself thinking bad thoughts, or find myself in a bit of a mood, one simple Mind Truth I use is... "I smile now, because now is my life." Saying this to myself interrupts myself, and gives me a clear focus for that moment. Another one I use is, "I smile and generate thoughts and feelings of peace, love, appreciation and enjoyment." I call this the Big Five, and I consciously and continuously program myself to live this.

Your mind can be your best friend or your worst enemy. Befriend it. Train it so it works *for* you, not against you. Train it to be happy. Programme it with what *you* want, not what *others* want for you. The majority of our thoughts, feelings, and actions occur without any conscious awareness or involvement. It's all automated. We need to make sure that what automatically comes up into the conscious mind is not debilitating, but life enhancing - thoughts of happiness, love, peace, confidence, success. Reprogramming ourselves using Mind Truths will help greatly.

Your Brilliant Mind

To prove how brilliant your mind is and how it works, have you ever forgotten someone's name, then while you're in the shower or doing something else, suddenly the name pops into your head? Your subconscious mind was working on it all the time, while your conscious mind was not. Your subconscious mind will work on your Mind Truths even after you've stopped doing them consciously. How good is that?

While you're doing your Mind Truths, think of it like building a house. Building work starts and effort is put in, but you are not living in it yet. As time goes on and your Mind Truths build in your head, the day will come when you live in these truths. You will be living in a new mind/house that you have built yourself to your own specifications.

When we have a definite belief embedded in the mind, the mind tends to reject ideas or information that conflicts with that belief. That's why some beliefs, even silly ones, can be persistent. But you can be even more persistent and can overcome old beliefs and old Mind Truths with new ones. Yes, the more we repeat a certain thought, the more real it becomes, which is what this book is all about. Once the new ones are embedded you will be consistently happier and feeling better.

Feeling The Words

Thoughts and words affect our physiology and feelings. Try this. Think of a time when something really funny happened to you or think of when someone or something made you laugh out loud. Really try to get into it by seeing what you saw at the time, hearing what you heard, and remembering how good you felt. If you're playing full out, you will now be smiling and feeling good. That's what this book's all about. By soaking your mind in positive Mind Truths, you'll feel better short term; and long term you'll build up the personality traits that you want to strengthen.

The more you repeat a word, the more your brain will search inwardly for experiences or situations that match that word. Try repeating one word, such as happiness, confidence, love, smile, appreciation or courage [silently or aloud] to yourself for a couple of minutes and see what happens.

Repetition Works

As Paul McKenna explains in his book, *I Can Make You Happy*, "You create habits by repetition. Each one of our thoughts and actions corresponds to a neural pathway in the brain. The more we repeat a thought or action, the stronger that pathway becomes just as a pathway across a field becomes more clear and firm the more people walk along it."

By repeating your Mind Truths, they will become embedded in your subconscious and become a permanent part of your personality. These Mind Truths will override many of the negative pathways present in your brain. They grow and become superhighways which permanently affect your subconscious mind, your conscious mind, and your actions for the better. You are upgrading your own software and it's far more important than upgrading your phone or TV or car.

Warning

When you start working on new Mind Truths, your mind may fight it. For example, you say, "I am bold and courageous," your mind may say, "Hey, what's this? This is not familiar. You're not bold and courageous. Do you remember when you were scared of a fly when you were four? When you were 10 you were scared of the bullies at school," etc, etc.» But with time and repetition of Mind Truths, the mind slowly gets it. It slowly gets the message and starts to embed it.

Your mind may resist the newness of something unfamiliar. It's simply trying to protect you from something which could be a threat. The answer is to make the unfamiliar familiar. After trying a new thing a few times, it becomes familiar and the resistance goes away. It becomes familiar and safe. If you find something is hard to do, don't say it's hard, say it's unfamiliar. It makes dealing with the situation much easier. If you're not used to praising yourself, encouraging yourself, believing in yourself, start doing it and it will become familiar and a part of you. Never criticise yourself or beat yourself up, rather forgive and encourage yourself. Praise boosts self-est teem, even if it comes from you. Be your own best friend.

Many of us have brains that are wired to return to the familiar. Have you seen children watching the same film or video over and over again? We tend to shop at the same shops and buy the same food and eat the same diet. If you feel resistance when it comes to doing this new system of Mind Truths, know that it's just your brain trying to get back to what's familiar.

Equally relevant is that when doing the same thing over and over, the brain can get bored and lose momentum, so we need to recognise this and make sure we stick to the new, unfamiliar method of doing the Mind Truths until it becomes a good habit.

Even if you don't initially believe a Mind Truth, if you repeat it often enough, the belief grows and it establishes itself. Your words, pictures, and beliefs are yours to change. Your mind is a tool for you to use for your own benefit. It's belongs to you and you can do what you want with it. Change your thoughts to change your feelings. Change your feelings to change your actions. Change your actions to change your results. Positive Mind Truths lead to beautiful, positive, results.

The good news about your physical brain is that you can grow new neurons (brain cells) and new neural pathways. The more you do your Mind Truths, the more your brain will grow. The sooner you get these Mind Truths embedded into your subconscious, the better. The more frequently and intensely you do them, the quicker the results.

Habits

The way to create a new habit, is simply to do a new action consistently for as long a period of time as necessary. Initially, a new activity will be unfamiliar and you may forget to do it or just give up because it's easier not to do it, than do it. But with a little consistency and perseverance, the habit is formed and then it's difficult to stop and the new habit is embedded in your being. Different people pick up new habits at different rates so don't compare yourself to anyone else. In time, it's easier to do the new habit than not do it. There's no trick to it. "Just do it," as Nike says. If you should miss, don't beat yourself up. Simply get back to it.

Repetition is the Mother of Skills

In order to learn any new activity or skill, it's necessary to do it again and again and again until it becomes familiar. How many times did you get on a two wheeler bike, before you could balance and go? How many times did you get in the water and splash about, before you could swim? It's the same with Mind Truths. We need to repeat them again and again and again until they are deeply ingrained in our minds. To upgrade your mind and life takes a little time and a little effort initially, until doing your Mind Truths becomes familiar and a habit, then they're easy to do and become a normal, effortless activity. Any effort incurred will pay handsome dividends for the rest of your life.

You know how you sometimes get a tune that keeps popping into your mind? You hardly notice it's there. Then you're suddenly aware of it. We want the same with our Mind Truths. For example, for a while every time I walked up some steps or stairs or an escalator, I would say to myself, "Strong and Powerful!" in a rhythmic way as I went up or down. Now whenever I go up or steps or stairs or an escalator it automatically comes into my mind. It's a neural habit and a good Mind Truth embedded.

The Subconscious Mind

The subconscious mind is running the show and is a repository of beliefs, habits, and actions which keep us living the way we do. If it wasn't running the show, we'd have to relearn how to walk, read, or drive a car every day. And it's powerful, as anyone who's tried to change an ingrained habit will know. But habits can be changed by creating new habits through repetition. Creating the habit of doing your Mind Truths rewards you with a master habit, which will effect other habits, as your Mind Truths catch hold and become embedded.

Strength In Numbers

If you can get your friends and family involved in Mind Truths too, there are many benefits. You get social confirmation that what you're doing is valid and worthwhile. Doing anything in a group or with a partner makes it easier and more fun. Seeing others get good results is motivating for you to keep doing it. You build stronger bonds in your relationships as you progress and grow together.

Here are a few Mind Truths about Mind Truths. Read them through a few times and allow them to start preparing your mind for the wonderful journey you are about to make, as you conquer anxiety, worry, fear and stress and master your life.

- I accept full responsibility for conquering my anxiety, worry, fear and stress.

- I believe Mind Truths are a great way to conquer my anxiety, worry, fear and stress.

- I believe Mind Truths are a great way to transform myself into the person I want to be.

- I do my Mind Truths every day to create the life of my dreams.

- Every day, in every way, I'm feeling better and better and better.

- I enjoy doing my Mind Truths.

- My Mind Truths upgrade my mind so I feel better and better.

- I allow Mind Truths to alter my mind and life for the better.

- I enthusiastically repeat my Mind Truths often and with feeling.

- I like my Mind Truths . I love my Mind Truths .

- As I do my Mind Truths I am becoming more relaxed, happier, more confident and more courageous.

CHAPTER 3

~

Training Your Beautiful Mind

The measure of intelligence is the ability to change. Albert Einstein

You cannot have a positive life and a negative mind. Joyce Meyer

The mind is everything. We are changed by our thoughts. What you think you become. Buddha

Fortune favours the prepared mind. Louis Pasteur

Yesterday I was clever, so I wanted to change the world. Today I am wise, so I am changing myself. Rumi

When you practice positive affirmations and keep your words and pictures consistent with your goals and dreams, there is nothing that can stop you being the success you are meant to be. Brian Tracy

Your mind only responds to two things: the pictures you make in your head and the words you say to yourself. And they are very easy to change. Marisa Peer

Self-suggestion is a powerful factor in building character... it is, in fact, the sole principle through which character is built. Napoleon Hill

If you focus on fears and doubts they become your inner reality, but when you immerse yourself in feelings and thoughts of love or peace or kindness towards others, these become your inner and outer reality. It will change your life. Mark Waldman

Self-talk means you tell yourself how to feel...how to respond. You literally say things in your mind or out loud to yourself... You have to give yourself affirmations. Brendon Burchard

Valuable and Important

Your mind is the most valuable and important thing you possess. Your mind is probably the most sophisticated and complex thing in the universe. Respect it. Own it. It is yours to use. Use it to your advantage.

Every thought matters

Your mind is magnificent. Your mind is constantly being stimulated by what goes on around you and within you.

Every thought you think, every situation you experience, everything you do, changes your mind for better or worse. It's up to you to change it for better.

You become what you think about most of the time, so think good, positive, upbuilding, uplifting, energising thoughts; rather than the often present negative, life debilitating thoughts. Negative thoughts are simply memories from the past influencing the present; or anticipation of bad things to come in the future. Recognise them for what they are: just thoughts. Recognise that you are not your thoughts. Be aware that you are the recogniser and observer of your thoughts. You and your thoughts are different. Your thoughts come, they go. Let the bad ones go quickly and hold onto the good ones longer. Your mind can't hold a negative and positive thought at the same time, so overpower the negative thoughts with positive, energising thoughts.

Your mind's Job

Your mind's primary job is to keep you safe, which it does by drawing your attention to anything that is potentially harmful or a threat. That's why bad news and misery sells, because your mind naturally pays attention to it, so you can avoid that situation in future. It's your hard wiring. It's your default setting. It's trying to protect you, guard you and look out for you. It's your ever present sentry and like any good look-out, it's constantly scanning for potential danger. "What's that noise?" "Careful on the road!" Watch that person!" "Don't do that. Stay in your comfort zone." Your mind runs on fear, worry and problems. No wonder we get stressed and run-down.

Your mind doesn't care whether you're happy or not; no threat. If you're full of love and joy and peace it can't do its job. Do you know anyone who isn't "happy" unless they are whingeing and complaining about their problems? Their mind is running their show.

You don't need to believe your thoughts. You don't need to accept as true every thought you think. By being aware of your thoughts you can evaluate their validity and choose to believe them or not; to act on them or not. This puts you in control of your mind. This means you live from conscious choice and not from the default, negative programming. Manage your own mind or your mind will manage you. Tame your own mind or your mind will tame you.

You can choose your own thoughts. This is how you take control and master your thoughts and yourself. This is how your mind becomes your supporter rather than your worst enemy. So train your mind. Work with it. Instruct it. Coach it. Educate it. Your mind learns by repetition, so drill it with the Mind Truths in this book. Master your mind with Mind Truths and watch your fears decrease and your confidence, courage and happiness increase.

Feel it

When your mind takes on a word, or picture, or thought, it also takes on the feelings associated with it. Whatever is going on in your mind triggers feelings. Because this is happening constantly and automatically we may not be so aware of it. Read these words and see if you register any feelings: death, hate, pain, kill, violence, torture. Not so nice! Shake them off and now try: peace, love, happiness, kindness, joy, appreciation, smiles. I hope you can feel the difference. You can consciously and actively avoid the thoughts, words, and pictures that are energy sapping disturbing and debilitating. Rather, consciously pour refreshing, energising and upbuilding thoughts, words and pictures into your mind until it overflows.

Recognise the difference between *move away from* states and *move towards* states. The *move away from* states are states we don't want to be in, such as fear, anger, depression and frustration. The *move towards* states are states we *do* want to be in, such as confidence, courage, peace, love, appreciation, happiness and enjoyment. Which states affect you? What do you want to move away from? What do you want to move towards?

Who's running your show?

If you think your conscious mind is running your show, think again. It's your subconscious mind. If you doubt that try changing an ingrained habit by conscious force. Try dieting, or giving up smoking, or giving up sex, drugs and rock and roll. Regardless of what you want consciously, your subconscious will fight you. To combat this I find it helpful to think of bad habits as simply being familiar to my mind, whereas things I want to change are simply unfamiliar to my mind. When changing behaviour, if you think of making bad things unfamiliar and good things familiar, it takes much of the anxiety out of change. By repeating the exercises in this book, your mind gets used to doing them, they become familiar, and a good habit is formed.

What's your job?

The mind quickly and easily defaults to daydream mode. Unfortunately it often refers back to negative past programming or anxieties of things to come in the future. Your job is to train your mind. Your job is to tell your mind what you want. Tell it great things. Your mind's job is to believe what you tell it. Repetition works. Tell it great things, again and again and again. Tell it encouraging things. It's simple, it's powerful and it works. Your mind lets in the good and bad alike, so you must choose to swap the bad with the good. Parents know that if their children play with the "bad" kids they'll be influenced by them. Don't let your mind play with "bad" debilitating thoughts. Rather let it play with the happy, good, positive, upbuilding, thoughts that benefit you. You are free to choose, so choose thoughts that encourage and energise you. Don't think of this as discovering yourself, think of it as creating yourself. Be the creator of your mind and life, not the manager of your circumstances. Decide to encourage and build yourself up to become exactly who you want to be.

It's science

Dr Bruce Lipton is a former medical school professor and research scientist. The fly-cover of his book, *The Biology of Belief*, states, "(His research) shows that genes and DNA do not control our biology; but instead DNA is controlled by signals from outside the cell, including the energetic messages emanating from our positive and negative thoughts." So as well as reprogramming our minds for the better, we can even influence how our DNA is expressed.

When I read a book or watch a program or lecture, I take notes in a way that I feel will serve me best. I'd like to include here the exact notes I took on watching one of Dr Lipton's lectures... "My mind controls my genes. My mind controls my life. I can change my mind and my life and biology. Also the environment controls the genes and biology and life. What I think controls my health. My body is just a reflection of what's going on in my mind. Change beliefs and attitudes about life I change my biology. Placebo/nocebo. Heal/kill. Don't be a victim of your belief system. Most of my thoughts are negative and abundant. Be aware and change the thoughts to positive ones. Life changer."

In conclusion, be aware of the thoughts going on in your mind. With awareness comes power. The power to choose. Your deciding to dismiss debilitating thoughts, while hanging onto positive thoughts, will change you for the better. You can program your mind with Mind Truths and become familiar with upbuilding, energising, thoughts and take your life to a higher level.

Read the Mind Truths below. Do it with feeling in an emotionally charged way for maximum benefit. Chapter 5 will give you suggestions as to different ways to use your Mind Truths.

Your Beautiful Mind Mind Truths

- My mind is the most valuable thing I have.

- My mind is the most beautiful and powerful thing in the universe.

- I am learning to control my mind.

- My mindset is my most important and valued asset.

- My mindset is changing anyway, so I make sure it changes in the direction I want.

- I am not my thoughts, but I am the observer of my thoughts.

- My greatest power is to choose my own thoughts. I look after my mind. I protect it from harmful input and I feed it positive input.

- I allow my bad mind habits to become unfamiliar to me, while I make new mind habits familiar.

- I let bad thoughts evaporate, but I hold on to good thoughts.

- I decide what to put in my mind and what not to put in my mind.

- My most important skill is being able to communicate with myself by programming my mind.

- I tell my mind what I want. I tell it great things.

- I appreciate that my mind is just trying to keep me safe, but I want to live in a happy, peaceful, confident, loving, appreciative, energised place.

- I train my mind or it will train me.

- I give clear direct instructions as to how I want my mind to operate. I become what I think about, so I think good, happy, encouraging, upbuilding, energising thoughts.

- My mind learns by repetition so I repeat my positive Mind Truths often.

- My Mind Truths change me. They change me internally in my mind and emotions; and externally in my actions.

- I absorb my Mind Truths like a sponge and allow them to positively influence me.

- I enjoy doing my Mind Truths.

CHAPTER 4

How to Conquer Anxiety, Worry, Fear and Stress.

As a rule, men worry about more about what they can't see, than about what they can see. Julius Caesar.

I don't worry about anything I can't control. That's a really good lesson in life. Tom Watson

Nothing in the affairs of men is worthy of great anxiety. Plato

We can easily forgive a child who is afraid of the dark. The real tragedy of life is when men are afraid of the light. Plato

Adapting the right attitude can convert a negative stress into a positive one. Hands Selye

Happiness is a choice. You can choose to be happy. There's going to be stress in life, but it's your choice whether you let it affect you or not. Valerie Bertinelli

The greatest weapon against stress is our ability to choose one thought over another. William James

There isn't a single day in life worth living in fear. Mo Gawdat

Conquer Anxiety, Worry, Fear and Stress.

After my bold, courageous and heroic act of buying Dale Carnegie's book, *How to Stop Worrying and Start Living*, I completely devoured it. I underlined it, marked it, highlighted it and read it so many times that the pages began to fall out. Before long the whole book fell apart and disintegrated. But I was hooked on self-improvement and went on to read many of the classics.

Life started to get better, and whenever it took a turn for the worse, there was always a self-development book to prop me up and give me hope. Things got really good when I built a successful network marketing business which brought in thousands of pounds a month. I was able to move from urban Manchester to the beautiful city of Exeter where I rented a stunning flat (apartment) overlooking the river. It was all going so well, until it started going so badly. Within a couple of years the money started to go down and it was obvious that the glory days were over, and things would just get worse and worse. My biggest fear was being broke. I wanted a life of freedom and choice and having a certain amount of money is essential.

As my income decreased, my anxiety, worry, fear and stress increased. I started having trouble getting off to sleep and would wake up earlier and earlier. Gradually the time I spent sleeping was less and less. During this time I started having panic attacks and lost the ability to drive. As a build up to the panic attacks I would pace like a frustrated, trapped lion in it's cage, except that my cage was my flat. I walked from the corner of the lounge out into the hall and then into the corner of my bedroom. Turn, then back again to the corner of the lounge. Turn, then back again. Repeat, repeat, repeat. This was a bad time in my life and I wouldn't wish it on anyone. This is certainly one of the reasons I wrote this book; in the hope of preventing this from happening to anyone else.

Anyway, the day came when I was convinced I wouldn't sleep at all that night. I was already in a terrible state and the thought of not sleeping at all was just the final straw. I took myself off to hospital and they gave me some drugs. These drugs put me to sleep. That was good, but the side-effects were terrible. After a couple of weeks I felt so bad on the drugs that I slowly weaned myself off them.

I ended up losing my beautiful flat and I ended up getting a job I hated. I slowly recovered though and during this period I used my Mind Truths a lot. At this time they were just a jumble of cards, but it occurred to me that if I could group them into subjects, I could simply pull out all the Mind Truths I had on that subject. It also occurred to me that since they helped me so much, they could also help others with similar problems and issues to me. That was three years ago and after much sorting, researching and writing, you now have the result in your hands; as regards the subject of anxiety, worry, fear and stress. Other subjects will follow. I hope this information and these Mind Truths will help you as much as they have helped me, and you won't end up going to dark places that you don't want to go to. Instead, you will be able to upgrade and master your life; to become the person you want to become and go to places that you really want to go to.

Understanding Your Adversary

It may help us to cope better, if we understand the differences between anxiety, worry, fear and stress. They all operate in a similar way and it may not matter what we call it when we are feeling terrible and anticipating pain. But understanding can be helpful, so let's split them up.

Worry is mainly going on in our minds. It is usually about something specific. It's not too debilitating and tends to be temporary since it stops when the trigger stops. eg. A father may be worried about his daughter who's out past her curfew time. But when the daughter gets in safe and sound, the worry stops.

Anxiety is what we feel as we anticipate a threat. It's an uneasy feeling of apprehension, of impending misfortune. It tends to be more general and maybe situational such as being anxious in crowds or open spaces. Anxious people may be generally anxious about things such as travelling or work or finances or health or their children. Anxiety can be a sociably acceptable term for fear.

Fear is a natural built in warning system which alerts us to potential or real danger. Walking down a dark alley at night may cause some fear, but it's only a potential danger. If a person jumps out with a knife demanding money, then it's a real danger. It is very good and healthy when a real danger is present as it prepares our bodies for action, but it's not so good when there is no real danger present. Fear is a feeling of agitation or dread in the face of this real or imagined danger. It can be looked on as rational fear or irrational fear. Rational fear is essential and useful as a protection mechanism which the body generates to warn us to be aware and take care. Irrational fear is not essential or useful and acts as a barrier to peace and success. Short periods of fear do little damage, if when the danger has passed we can stand down, relax, and allow the body to recover. However if the fear becomes continuous, it results in stress, which is very damaging to the mind and body.

Stress is a disruption to a relaxed body, by keeping us in long term fight or flight state. Stress is tension, a pressure, a tightness, a tautness, a state of physical, mental or emotional strain resulting from a danger, potential danger, or being under too much mental or emotional pressure. When we need something to turn out the way we want, but don't think we can control it and we anticipate it going badly, that's stressful. Anything that poses a challenge or threat to our well-being can be a stressor. Stress can be a socially acceptable term for fear.

It's not all bad

Stress isn't all bad. Some of the latest ideas are that stress is only harmful to health if you believe it is. Also stress can be a useful message that you're entering into unknown territory. It's not a stop sign but rather a warning sign. So proceed with awareness and caution. Physically stress can energise you and prepare you to meet that challenge. Stress can also warn you that something needs to change. You may need to change the meaning of something or actually change something in your life. Stress in the body which creates illness and disease means something needs to be changed to get your body back into a non-stressed, relaxed, healthy state. If stress is the result of a problem, then acknowledging the problem and looking for solutions and implementing them solves the problem and stops the stress. Just moving towards a solution and making progress can take much stress out of the situation. Progress feels good and releases pressure, even if the problem is still there.

Any time you take risks you're likely to feel anxious however, a positive aspect of this is that if you do what you're scared of doing it expands who you are as a person. And it gets results.

Mind control

One aspect of fear is looking into the crystal ball in our minds and imagining a bad situation happening. What's the opposite? Looking into the crystal ball of our minds and imagining a good situation happening. Both are able to be conjured up voluntarily. Which is better? It's your choice. You're in control of your mind. It may not always be easy, but it's an option worth playing with. I don't know if this book will be a best seller, but I do know writing this book could be stressful if I focused on the time and effort needed to do an outstanding job; and then think that after all that hard work people won't like it and it doesn't sell. I prefer to imagine that it *will* be a best seller and help hundreds of thousands, maybe millions, of people to improve their lives. There is no reality here, only a deliberate mindset of optimism and intention. I decide how to view the situation.

Another way of looking at it is that fear comes from focus, so don't focus on the bad things happening in your life. To be fearful you must be thinking fearful thoughts. Focus instead on the good things that have happened in the past. Focus on what's good about your present life today. Focus on the good that you want to happen in the future.

Threat or challenge?

There is a big difference between a real threat to our wellbeing, where there is danger of injury or death, and the challenge of doing something new or outside your comfort zone, which may go bad for you. Public speaking is a classic example. To conquer this and other fears, it's helpful to think of the feeling as, not stress, but excitement and then commit to doing your relaxed best. It's interesting to note that fear and excitement are very similar feelings in the body. When you see people screaming on a rollercoaster are they fearful or excited, or maybe a bit of both? So next time you feel a little scared say to yourself, "This is exciting, stimulating, arousing, thrilling." Simply be excited.

Knowing what resources you bring to any situation is important. If you have enough resources to cope with the stress, it becomes a challenge. If you don't have enough you need to find the resources, the knowledge, the skills to move on and succeed.

What does it mean?

When something bad happens it can be very stressful especially if you focus on the loss. You split up with your boyfriend/ girlfriend and it's the end of the world. When something happens that really upsets you, how do you react? This tested me when I got sacked from a job I wanted to keep. Out of the blue, after being there three months, I was called into the boss's office and told I didn't fit in. "Goodbye and don't come in tomorrow." I was shocked, upset, angry and stressed. But after a couple of hours I decided to "reframe" the situation and look at it differently. First of all, some of the people there were very unpleasant which I didn't like, and the work wasn't that fulfilling either. So I decided it was a great opportunity to find a better job. I applied myself to this and I ended up getting a better job with less hours which gave me more time to write this book. Because I gave the situation a new meaning, changed my perception and interpretation of the events, my stress went and I freed my mind to look for and move onto better things.

Bigger problems

We all have problems and they will likely continue until the day we die. Could it be that the higher your quality of problem the higher and greater the quality of your life? If you have little problems that stress you out, maybe you're not playing the game of life at a high enough level. If you are stressed because someone cut you up in traffic or was rude to you, maybe it's time to get bigger problems that challenge you and move you on.

Believe it or not!

Anxiety comes from believing our thoughts. Your feelings are created by your thoughts, not the event. You are not your thoughts. You are what's creating your thoughts. If you think when you get on a plane it will crash, that's real anxiety. If you are aware of these thoughts, you can dismiss them and replace them with positive thoughts, such as having a great time at your destination. You are not your thoughts. Be aware that you are not your thoughts. Instead be the observer of your thoughts. Thoughts come and go but you remain throughout. You can choose to dismiss disquieting thoughts and replaced them with good, optimistic, beneficial ones.

Another thing to do when disquieting thoughts come up is to imagine stepping outside of yourself, where you can observe yourself and your thoughts and the situation, as a curious bystander would. This can ease much of the stress.

Wired for fear.

We are wired for fear. We are wired for survival. Your mind has no interest in your happiness, which is unimportant for your survival. You will fight or flee if there is a real threat to you, so you can fight or flee another day. Your mind is constantly looking for areas of threat or lack so it can bring it to your attention, so you can do something about it and survive. In any situation you'll notice that your mind has this tendency; to spot what's wrong and what can represent a threat. No wonder we get stressed. Today the threat no longer comes from marauding tribes or wild animals or starvation, but from the media, (especially the news), money issues, health issues, relationship issues and such like.

If you mull over the possibility that something terrible could happen, the brain releases stress chemicals to prepare the body to fight or flee. If this becomes frequent and continuous it can seriously damage the brain and even lead to panic attacks and a nervous breakdown.

Reframing negative thoughts and threats.

Problems can cause much stress, but don't fall into the trap of learnt helplessness. How we view a problem makes a huge difference to how it affects us. Ask yourself the 4 Ps. 1) Personal. Is the problem I have my fault alone? 2) Pervasive. Is my whole life just this problem? 3) Permanent. Will this problem last for ever? 4) Powerless. Is a solution completely beyond me? Answering yes to any of these questions indicates learned helplessness. To overcome it and move on, be strong, be courageous, be responsible, be resourceful, try different solutions, make better choices, create possibilities, take action. Never give up.

Stress as a Joy Stealer

Since your mind seeks safety, when you are worried or stressed it's has no use for the pleasure systems of your body and it shuts them down. It can even be difficult to enjoy the company of others and enjoy a conversation with them. Focusing on what brings pleasure and satisfaction, and resolving the problems you have can help you access joy and happiness again.

Take action

Sometimes what we most fear doing is what we need to do. It's the fear of the unknown outcome that prevents us from taking action. It helps if you decide what the worst case results could be, accept it as a slight possibility, then do all in your power to prevent this worst case from happening.

There is often more pain in not taking action, than actually taking it. If you are willing to do the thing you fear, you expand and grow as a person. And you feel so much better for it after it's happened. The cost of bowing to fear and inaction is your life. Develop the most important habit of those who excel and succeed; take action.

Inbuilt fears and not being enough.

We are born with only two inbuilt fears. The fear of falling and the fear of loud noises. All others are learnt. One of the biggest fears we learn as we grow up is, "I'm not enough." Not enough as a person, not lovable enough, not skilled enough, not loved enough, not good-looking enough, not...enough. (Fill in the blank) this leads to poor self-esteem which can be very stressful. You can combat this by repeating frequently to yourself, "I am enough, I like myself, I love myself."

Other people

There may be times when you're dealing with a difficult person and it's causing you stress. A quick and easy hack is to imagine them wearing only their underwear and a funny hat. Just be careful you don't start smiling or laughing inappropriately.

What's your fear?

People are afraid of all sorts of things. Here are a few of them: failure, rejection, spiders, heights, death, the dark, public speaking, commitment, not being lovable, being poor, criticism, old age, loneliness, sickness /disease, redundancy, the future, conflict, being judged, not being loved, loss of loved ones, being attacked, open spaces, closed spaces. Check to see if any of these are pertinent to you. Ask yourself, "What am I afraid of?" Know yourself and know that if fear is allowed to remain in you you will never feel totally safe, free and joyful. Do whatever you can to get rid of these fears. Use this book or find help wherever you can. Beat fear and enjoy your life to the full.

Mental Solutions. Hacks to Conquer Stress

- Do the Mind Truths in this book.

- Think of fear as having a purpose, namely that it provides extreme focus.

- Remind yourself not to believe every thought that comes into your head. You are not your thoughts. You are separate from your thoughts. You are the creator and observer of your thoughts. Replace a bad thought with a better one; a good, encouraging, upbuilding one.

- Write your own Mind Truths on subjects such as, peace, confidence, taking responsibility, happiness, smiling, love, appreciation, courage, self-esteem, forgiveness, enjoyment.

- Be excited. The next time you feel a little scared say to yourself, "This is exciting, stimulating, arousing, thrilling." Simply be excited.

- Take a reality check. Knowing that, "This too shall pass," takes much of the angst out of it.

- If you come to the present moment, there is normally no danger or threat to your presence. Fear is about tomorrow so beat it by living today and being in the present moment. Live in the now.

- Remember a situation or time when you felt really good. When you felt love, joy, connection, happiness, peace. See the scene, hear what was going on and really get into how you felt.

- Do a relaxation exercise. There are plenty on the Internet.

- Since the brain is always vigilant and scanning for potential threats you may sometimes feel an undercurrent of anxiety. You can actually talk to your brain. Reassure it that things are safe. Tell it things like, "No threats here. Let's move on. We're safe," Encourage it to stand down.

- Be the observer. If you imagine stepping outside of yourself to observe yourself and the situation from a detached perspective, you can be less attached to your worries, anxieties and fears. It's much easier to cope with the situation when you're not in it mentally and emotionally. Take the situation seriously but not personally.

- Learn to meditate. Very relaxing and centring.

- Remember that much suffering comes when you're preoccupied with yourself. We are all self-centred at times, but focusing on appreciating what we have, and loving and helping others can alleviate much anguish.

- Fear and appreciation can't exist in the mind at the same time, so do appreciation when stressed; and at other times.

- Ask yourself empowering questions when stressed such as, "What good could come out of this?" "What can I learn from this situation?" "How can I make the situation even better than before?"

- Close your eyes and imagine doing something you enjoy. Since we can only hold one thought at a time, this can reduce or replace feelings of anxiety.

- Think of a value based word that could help you deal with the stress you're in such as joy, peace, happiness, progress, love, relax, forgive, confidence, energy, smile, courage. Keep repeating that one word for a minute or two or longer and see what happens!

Physical Solutions. Hacks to Conquer Stress

- Breathe deeply. Take several deep breath's right down into your belly.

- Open your mouth wide and force a yawn a few times.

- Close your eyes and look up towards your eyebrows. You may put your eyes into REM (rapid eye movements) which is good. Hold this and think of pleasant thoughts.

- Change your environment. (e.g. go for a walk/meet a friend/go to a cafe. Go to the cinema or theatre or dancing or play a sport. Buy a ticket and go watch something)

- Exercise – Exercising helps take your mind off things. It also disperses tension from the muscles. Being fit makes you more resilient to stress.

- Practice box breathing. Slowly breath in to the count of four. Hold that breath for the count of four. Exhale slowly to the count of four. Hold that exhale for the count of four. Do at least a couple of minutes. As it becomes familiar and easier, increase to the count of five or six or seven or beyond.

- Do something you enjoy. Distract yourself. Things may look different afterwards.

- Smile. Make it real. Soften your eyes and lips. (Think of something that makes you smile while you do this.) If necessary put a pen or pencil horizontally between your lips. You look silly and it forces you to smile.

- If anxiety is a signal to do something, taking action to overcome the problem clears much of that anxiety. Solve that problem!

- To avoid overload, chunk a big problem down into smaller and smaller tasks which are now manageable. Only concern yourself with the task in hand, not the whole task.

- Be physically healthy. Your body can cope better with stress if it works properly. Also poor health itself can itself be a stressor. Weight training is especially beneficial.

- Take a weekend break or holiday. Take time to recuperate and recover.

- Find something to laugh at; Jokes, films, audios, TV, radio, internet, podcasts, whatever works for you. Humour is great because it tells the mind, "Nothing to fear here, relax and enjoy."

CHAPTER 5

~

How to Use Your Mind Truths

Please don't think that reading through this book once will transform your life. It will take a little time and a little effort. But it will be worth it. You are constantly changing anyway. You may as well change in the direction you choose, set your own sails, be your own captain. Instruct your beautiful mind to take you to new, exciting places. Mind Truths are to be repeated often and with emotional feeling while you are confident that they are going into and changing your mind. At Romans 12:2 the Bible says, "Stop being moulded by this system of things, but be transformed by making your mind over…" Don't let other people and their ideas (this system) mould you. Transform and mould yourself. Build yourself up. Be actively reinventing yourself for the better.

Be aware that your mind may play tricks on you, if it wants you to stay the same; but you must be ruthless. Take control. Do what needs to be done to get the results you want. Prime your mind. Overwhelm your mind with positive Mind Truths, in the area you want to improve in. Practice, practice, practice. Repeat, repeat, repeat. Make doing your Mind Truths a habit. Repeat your Mind Truths until they become a habit. The more power, feeling and energy you put into them, the quicker and easier they will grow.

Below are different ways you can do your Mind Truths. Make it as easy as you can. Do which ever of them that you think will be most doable and most fun.

Don't be overwhelmed if you feel there are too many Minds Truths. Simply choose a number that you can cope easily with and work with these. I sometimes work with one or two cards worth. It works well for me. It makes it easy and very doable.

If you are feeling stressed before you do these Mind Truths, you will find that as you do them your mind has to focus on what it's doing and shut down the negative thoughts thus giving instant relief. This works even better when you say them aloud. This works even better if you do them with someone else since part of your focus will be on them. Also helping other people is a great stress reliever.

1) Read the Mind Truths from the book silently, but with energy and feeling.

2) Read the Mind Truths from the book with emotion, but hearing the words in your head. ie, speaking them silently to yourself.

3) Read the Mind Truths aloud with feeling.

4) Read the Mind Truths aloud with feeling while pacing the room, with attitude. Or while you're outside enjoying nature.

5) Copy or print out the relevant Mind Truths, so you easily have them to hand.

6) Write your Mind Truths on 3 x 5 cards and keep them together with a rubber band. Your writing hand is connected directly to your brain. According to Dan Sullivan, 40% of the brain is connected to that hand. So this is a very valid and effective strategy for your transformation. Write in the colour ink you think will imprint on your mind most firmly. Write in your best, neatest handwriting. This sends a powerful message to your mind that you're serious about this, that this is important. When I use words such as great, fantastic, wonderful, if you can think of a better word which resonates more strongly with you, use your word not mine. Read your Mind Truths frequently. Energise your day by doing them

first thing in the morning. Even before you get out of bed, perhaps. Do them in bed last thing at night before going to sleep. Do them many times during the day. Use 'dead' time such as while commuting, between activities, on public transport or as a passenger in a car. Involve the driver. Do them while waiting around. You could time how long it takes to do them once, so you know the time commitment for each reading. You could set a timer to go off every hour or two or three to remind yourself to do them. If you feel there are too many Mind Truths to cope with try this. Write them all out on 3 x 5 cards anyway, then decide how long to read them for, say two or five minutes. Set a timer and do your cards for two to five minutes, then stop regardless of how many you've read. Next time just continue from where you left off. This way you will cycle through your Mind Truths nice and easily. Alternatively you could pick out your top 10 or top 20 Mind Truths, write them on your cards and work with them. Keep your cards on your person so they are easily accessible when you have a free moment to do them in.

7) Record the Mind Truths you're working on, (on your phone maybe) then play them back to yourself frequently.

8) Find a friend or family member to do the Mind Truths aloud with you.

A) One person reads one line and the other person reads the next line.

B) One person reads one line then the other person reads the same line.

C) One person reads one line then the other person repeats the line without reading it. Swap

D) One person reads one line and the other person says it back to them in the second person. eg, First person "I am enough. I like myself. I love myself." Second person, "You are enough. You like yourself. You love yourself." Swap.

9) See if you can memorise some of your Mind Truths, then you can say them silently or aloud to yourself any time you want.

10) Teachers: Do the Mind Truths with your pupils. Create classes around Mind Truths

11) Parents: Do appropriate mind truths with your children. It's good bonding and great for their development.

A) Read appropriate Mind Truths to young children at bedtime.

B) Use them as a teaching aid to help them learn to read.

C) Record the Mind Truths you want to install in them with your voice and using their name in the 2nd person. They are sure to play it often.

D) If children need practice in writing, have them write out relevant Mind Truths. What could be better for them? If you yourself use cards they may want to have their own cards.

Be aware of how you feel before you start your Mind Truths. Notice how you feel after doing them. You'll likely be feeling much better and more confident in your chosen area.

CHAPTER 6

Mind Truths

How to Conquer Anxiety, Worry, Fear and Stress

- I do not allow anxiety, worry, fear or stress to hold me back or inhibit me.

- If I can't influence it or change it, I accept it and move on.

- I let go of the past. It's finished, over with. I move on.

- I mentally accept the worst that could happen, but then I do all I can to bring about the best that could happen.

- If something scares me, there's magic on the other side.

- I am bigger than my problems and challenges.

- Action is where the action is. Action diminishes fear. I take action.

- Despite any worry, fear, doubt, inconvenience or discomfort I take action.

- Life is sometimes tough, but I am tougher.

- Real growth comes through intense, difficult and challenging situations.

- I change what can be changed and accept what can't be changed.

- I am not my thoughts. I am the creator and observer of my thoughts.

- I detach myself from my thoughts and situations so I can observe them from outside of myself.

- I have the ability to create good thoughts, and I do.

- Fear comes from bad focus, so I don't focus on the bad things happening in my life. I focus on the good things that have happened in the past. I focus on what's good about my life today. I focus on the good I want to happen in the future.

- I don't see fearful things as threats, rather as challenges.

- I don't fear change. I welcome change. Change creates opportunity and progress and growth.

- The most adaptable people thrive, so I adapt well to new situations and I thrive.

- I perceive the world as a safe place for me to enjoy and play.

- I don't fear failure. Failure is an opportunity to learn and to begin again more intelligently.

- There is no failure, only learning.

- Fear is about tomorrow. I beat it by living today.

- I have the ability to cope with challenging or threatening situations. I cope well and thrive.

- I live from choice in the moment, rather than programming from the past.

- If fearful thoughts come up, I thank my mind for trying to protect me. I reassure it, "No threat here. Let's move on." Then I focus on encouraging thoughts.

- I am cool, calm and collected.

- While experiencing a challenging situation, I remember that this too will pass.

- I am aware that everything changes and I remember this and thrive.

- Much of what I feared in the past, never happened.

- Much of what I fear in the future, will never happen.

- I pay attention to the dialogue playing in my head and if necessary I change it to positive Mind Truths.

- I am a coper. I have great coping skills. I cope brilliantly with challenging situations.

- Whatever life throws at me, I can manage.

- I've experienced times of fear and stress in the past and got through it. I'll get through it now.

- I don't worry about the problem. I work on the solution.

- I don't wish things were easier for me. I wish I was stronger, and I work on this. I get stronger and stronger every day.

- When issues arrive I ask, "What's the lesson and gift in this for me?"

- I do not fear being different. I am unique and authentic. I accept myself. Other people accept me too.

- I do not try to change other people. I accept them exactly as they are.

- I am enough. I like myself. I love myself.

- Life is too short to suffer. I flourish instead.

- I don't do fear. I do excitement.

- Stressful situations are always temporary. I get through them. I cope. I thrive.

- I don't fear rejection. I expect acceptance.

- I don't fear failure. I take intelligent risks.

- I learn from failure. I fall forward and bounce back up.

- I recover quickly from adversity. I am emotionally resilient.

- Challenges are temporary, but my resilience is permanent.

- I do not fear looking foolish. I put myself out there, and do what I think is right and proper. People respect this.

- I do not compare myself to others. I am unique and different to every other person on the planet.

- I do not fear criticism. I am confident enough of my own opinions and actions.

- I do not fear being judged. I am confident enough to judge myself positively.

- I do not fear being unloved. I am lovable and loved. I love myself and other people love me too.

- Other people love me because I'm authentically my-self and I make them feel good about themselves.

- I maintain my composure at all times.

- I don't allow myself to get upset with other people. I am in control. I accept them exactly as they are. I keep calm. I am unmessablewith. I am unshakable. I forgive. I let go and move on.

- I can imagine that difficult people are only wearing their underwear and funny hats.

- I love my mind and body. I nurture them and give them relaxation and recovery time.

- I am fully and completely relaxed. I maintain my com-posure and keep calm at all times.

- I do not allow anxiety, worry, fear or stress to run my life. I control them well. I am in control.

- I am safe. I feel safe. My environment is safe.

- I curiously look forward to a calm, peaceful, fun, future.

- I deserve a better present and a better future.

- I feel safe and secure as I cultivate my love-based emotions.

- I trust in myself, my talents and my abilities, as I deserve and anticipate a wonderful future.

- Every day in every way I'm feeling better and better.

- Appreciation, love and action diminish fear.

- As I move away from fear I cultivate my confidence and courage.

- As I move away from fear, I move towards peace, love, appreciation and enjoyment.

CHAPTER 7

Helping Yourself and Helping Others

Are you pleased with the contents of this book? Do you feel it has given you good value? Have you learnt something new? Are you changing? Has your time with the book, been time well spent? I certainly hope so, and I'd like to think I have succeeded in helping you become closer to the person you want to be. I hope you enjoy using this book, as much as I enjoyed writing it. And I hope you continue to work with your various Mind Truths, as I still do.

I must congratulate you for finishing this book, however it's not really the finish, but rather a new beginning. As we know change can be difficult. Wanting to change, but not knowing how, is most frustrating. You are now in the know. You have in your hands a very simple but fun, workable system for upgrading and mastering your life. Use it, work it, keep at it, and your life will be changed for ever. And so will the lives of those you touch.

If you would like to get in touch with me I'd be delighted to hear how this book with its Mind Truths have affected your life. You can contact me through my website paulbooth.org.

After you have conquered anxiety, worry, fear and stress, what's next? Consider getting the next book in this series so you can master your confidence and courage.

Giving of yourself and contributing to the well-being of others is a fine thing to do. It brings much happiness to the giver as well as the receiver. It's a win win. It is my passion and purpose to spread more peace, love, appreciation, enjoyment and well-being through my books and public speaking. I invite you to help me do this. In doing so you spread more happiness and well-being in your own world. You could do six things...

1) Do you know anyone who is stressed? You could buy a copy of this book for them. They are sure to appreciate it.

2) Help others by involving them in the exercises in this book. It will of course help you too.

3) Recommend this book to your friends and social network.

4) Do you have any contacts with any schools, colleges, universities, educational establishments, charities, associations, clubs, companies, organisations, events, conventions, etc? Please send me their details. Or suggest they get in touch with me so we can see how I can help their people.

5) Put a book review on Amazon. The more comments there are on Amazon the more likely people are to consider the book (and check it out for themselves). I would be very grateful and appreciate it if you would do this. I thank you in advance.

6) Also, you could buy this book as a present for family, friends, colleagues and anyone you know. Not only is this a great present everyone will appreciate, it solves the problem of what to buy people for birthdays, Christmas, anniversaries, engagements, weddings, births, Hanukkah, Mother's Day, Father's Day, Valentine's Day, retirement, congratulations, prizes, to say thank you; expressions of love or friendship; expressions of gratitude or appreciation; or just because...

Finally, and in conclusion, may I thank you for reading and using this book, and may I wish you a life of much confidence, much courage, much peace, much fun, much happiness, much love, much appreciation, and much enjoyment.

Made in the USA
Middletown, DE
12 May 2020